A Jury Blinded

The Case of Colin Norris

Inside Justice

A Jury Blinded by Science - The Case of Colin Norris
ISBN 978-0-9562855-8-4

First edition published 2013 by: Inside Justice
Botley Mills,
Botley
Southampton
Hampshire SO30 2GB

Contents

1. Introduction

On 3rd March 2008 at Newcastle Crown Court **Colin Norris** was convicted of murder and attempted murder after a trial which lasted nineteen weeks. He received a life sentence with a recommendation that he serve a minimum of 30 years in prison. The prosecution case was that while working as a nurse at two Leeds hospitals he unlawfully injected insulin into five elderly female patients causing them to suffer severe hypoglycaemia (low blood sugar). Four of the women died. None of them had diabetes. The Crown argued that Colin Norris was the *'common denominator'* in all five cases as he had been on duty when the patients' low blood sugar had developed. It was further claimed that severe hypoglycaemia in non-diabetic patients was so rare that it could only be explained by a massive dose of insulin or other diabetic medication having been administered externally.

Colin Norris was dubbed the *'Angel of Death'* in the press. From the moment he was first arrested in 2002, he has protested his innocence. The case against him was based on a widely-held fallacy. Far from being a rare occurrence, new studies indicate that hypoglycaemia is relatively common among elderly hospital patients with conditions other than diabetes. This evidence has never been considered by any court.

The lengthy West Yorkshire Police inquiry into the alleged crimes of Colin Norris was headed by senior officers who had recently reviewed the case of serial killer Dr. Harold Shipman. The failure of neighbouring Greater Manchester Police to apprehend Shipman earlier was strongly criticised by Dame Janet Smith in her official report on the case. Since Colin's conviction, senior police officers have repeatedly asserted they 'stopped another Harold Shipman in the making'[1]. By their own admission, the West Yorkshire inquiry team speculated that Colin Norris was a serial killer before they had plausible concrete evidence. From the outset, their bias was to investigate 'deaths in which the suspect Norris had attended at the time'[2]. His case demonstrates the extreme danger that conclusion-driven police investigations may lead to the conviction of innocent people.

The case also illustrates difficulties posed by the manner in which expert opinion evidence is presented within the adversarial trial system. The fact that evidence from expert witnesses constitutes opinion may be overlooked to be replaced by trust in the erroneous notion of scientific certainty. After months of such testimony, the jury at the trial of Colin Norris may have felt 'blinded by science'.

Having considered the facts, we hope you will agree that Colin Norris has been the victim of a grave miscarriage of justice which must be corrected.

note: Individuals not previously named in media reports are identified
         by initials in this booklet.

---

[1] Hepworth M. *Operation Bevel: An Insight on how to manage a multi-death investigation in a health care setting* Journal of Homicide and Major Incident Investigation Vol. 7 Issue 1 Spring 2011

[2] ibid

2. Ethel Hall

On 11th November 2002, retired shopkeeper **Ethel Hall** aged 86 was admitted to Ward 36 - a mixed orthopaedic ward - at Leeds General Infirmary (LGI) with a broken hip after a fall at her home. She underwent an operation to repair the fracture on 14th November 2002. While she showed signs of mental confusion before and after surgery, she appeared to be making a satisfactory physical recovery.

Mrs. Hall had suffered from pernicious anaemia for more than 20 years. She had a long history of spontaneously losing consciousness for which no cause had ever been determined. During the daytime on 19th November 2002, she was found by a Health Care Assistant slumped to one side, unresponsive but still breathing while using a commode behind a screen. She was given oxygen and recovered consciousness. A doctor concluded she had experienced a syncopal (fainting) attack. This episode was mentioned to the Ward 36 night duty nursing team so that they could keep a particular eye on her.

The night team - whose shift lasted from 20.45 until 07.45 - comprised two staff nurses including Colin Norris and a Health Care Assistant supervised by a Nurse Practitioner who covered several wards.

That evening, Mrs. Hall complained she was in pain. She was given the painkiller Co-proxamol and later - on the prescription of a House Officer doing her ward rounds – a stronger analgesic Tramadol. Mrs. Hall had been confused and agitated during the early part of the night shift. She removed her bedcovers and nightshirt and tried to get out of bed. Later, she seemed to have settled. Observation records completed at various times during the night show nothing remarkable. However, at around 5.00 am, she was heard making loud choking noises. The night team went to her assistance. Staff Nurse Norris took charge and applied suction equipment to her mouth to remove any potential blockages but nothing came out. He also tested her cardiac condition, blood pressure and oxygen levels. He applied an oxygen mask and her oxygen levels started to rise.

Leeds General Infirmary

Doctors were summoned. Mrs. Hall was examined by the House Officer. Suspecting possible opioid overdose (both of the analgesic drugs she had been given are in the opioid category), the doctor discussed with a more experienced Clinical Fellow whether to inject Mrs. Hall with an antidote drug Naloxone. He agreed this was the appropriate treatment and she was injected with the drug. The Clinical Fellow came to the ward and examined Mrs. Hall who remained unresponsive. His diagnosis was that she was suffering from either opioid poisoning, hypoglycaemia (low blood sugar) or a stroke. The House Officer tried to summon the on-call medical team but they were already with a patient in another ward and could not attend. While she was on the telephone to the on-call team, Staff Nurse Norris told her Mrs. Hall's blood sugar was 1.5 mmol/L. This was a dangerously low level.

HYPOGLYCAEMIA

The brain requires glucose to function. The concentration of glucose (sugar) in a person's blood is expressed in millimoles per litre (mmol/L). A blood sugar concentration below 4.0 mmol/L may be considered hypoglycaemic although symptoms usually do not occur until the level has fallen below 3.0 mmol/L. Severe hypoglycaemia if untreated may result in unconsciousness, irreversible brain damage and death. A standard treatment for hypoglycaemia is to administer glucose orally or through injection via a cannula or venflon (small tubes inserted into a vein).

The largest group who experience hypoglycaemia are people with diabetes who inject insulin or who take anti-diabetic drugs called sulfonylurea. An excess of such medication may cause blood sugar to fall too low. For this reason people with diabetes are advised to test their blood sugar several times daily and to carry glucose in the form of dextrose tablets. Hypoglycaemia, however, is not confined to people with diabetes. Other factors may cause blood sugar to fall to dangerously low levels.

Mrs. Hall's death

Among other possibilities, doctors speculated that Mrs. Hall might have received an injection of insulin by mistake. At around 6.00 am, she was given the first of several glucose administrations in an attempt to increase her blood sugar and bring her out of coma. Her blood glucose concentration was checked at regular intervals. She received 600g of glucose in eleven doses over 36 hours. Although her blood sugar rose to normal after two hours, she did not regain consciousness. Doctors were puzzled by her hypoglycaemia for which there was no obvious explanation.

Blood tests carried out in the hospital's laboratory ruled out various potential diagnoses. A consultant in geriatric medicine instructed that a sample of Mrs. Hall's blood be sent to a specialist laboratory, Supra-Regional Assay Service (SAS) based at the Royal Surrey County Hospital in Guildford. The Guildford laboratory was able to measure the amount of insulin and also the level of a protein called c-peptide. When the pancreas produces insulin naturally, c-peptide is also created in similar amounts. Insulin injected by people with diabetes does not contain c-peptide. The presence of insulin in a sample with no c-peptide may indicate it was administered via injection rather than being produced by the pancreas.

On 29th November 2002, the hospital was informed that the Guildford laboratory's test showed a very high concentration of insulin in her blood (in excess of 12,000 picomoles[3] per litre) with no c-peptide. This result, it was claimed, could only be due to injection of a large amount of insulin. There are, however, questions surrounding the Guildford laboratory test as outlined in the next chapter. The hospital authorities contacted West Yorkshire Police who began an investigation on 6th December 2002. At around this time, the doctor who had taken Mrs. Hall's blood sample contacted the Medical Defence Union which provides legal support for medical staff whose clinical competence is challenged.

Meanwhile, Mrs. Hall had been transferred on 21 November to another ward within the hospital. In the early hours of 11th December 2002, she was pronounced dead. A *post mortem* examination concluded that she had suffered brain damage consistent with severe hypoglycaemia.

---

[3] A measurement of extremely small amounts of a substance. One picomole is one billionth of a millimole.

3. The Guildford Result

The result of analysis of Mrs. Hall's blood sample prompted West Yorkshire Police's investigation and later formed a key component of the Crown's case against Colin Norris. Aspects of the immunoassay[4] carried out by the Guildford laboratory on Mrs. Hall's blood are puzzling.

Blood samples were taken from Mrs. Hall at 6.00 am on 20th November 2002. At some time after 8.00 am, the hospital's laboratory was asked if these samples could be tested for insulin and c-peptide. The laboratory advised that the specific tests require samples to be frozen immediately. If kept at room temperature, insulin in the sample would become unstable within 1-3 days. The 6.00 am sample had not been frozen. The laboratory suggested fresh samples be taken and brought to them for freezing and despatch by courier to Guildford. This was done at 11.00 am some six hours after Mrs. Hall had been discovered in a hypoglycaemic state. By this time, her blood sugar had risen to a normal level (4.2 mmol/L).

C-Peptide test
The biochemist in charge of the Guildford laboratory initially stated on '22nd November 2002 *the sample was analysed for insulin and c-peptide'*. On 27th July 2003, he changed his statement:

> *when the Ethel Hall sample was tested by my laboratory on 22nd November 2002, the sample was only tested for insulin*

---

[4] A laboratory procedure for measuring the amount of a substance in a sample

and not c-peptide as originally stated…the sample was again tested on 27th November 2002. On this occasion it was tested for both insulin and c-peptide.

Given that the sample was sent specifically to test for insulin and c-peptide, it is unclear why the c-peptide test was not carried out straight away and why five days elapsed before it was effected. At Colin's trial, the biochemist could not recall why he only tested the sample for insulin on 22nd November. No satisfactory explanation was given for this omission.

No second test
If an unusual or unexpected result is obtained during scientific analysis, it is standard practice to check the result by running the test again using a second sample and – if possible – different equipment. The Guildford result from Mrs. Hall's sample pointed to the highly unusual finding that she had received a huge external dose of insulin. Despite this, no second test was conducted or apparently even contemplated.

At Colin's trial, **Dr Gwen Wark**, a biochemist who assisted in the analysis, said there was no need to repeat the test because the result was consistent with the administration of insulin.

Insulin Autoimmune Syndrome
The result reported by the Guildford laboratory would also have been consistent with an extremely rare condition called Insulin Autoimmune Syndrome (IAS). This possibility could have been excluded (or confirmed) by testing for an antibody[5] called IgM. An inexpensive test to detect IgM and other antibodies had been used by the same laboratory in the past and would have only taken a few hours. No such test was

---

[5] A protein produced within the body which identifies and neutralises foreign objects such as bacteria and viruses

carried out on Mrs. Hall's sample. At trial, Dr Wark said the test for IgM and other antibodies was not run because they required further samples and Mrs. Hall did not survive long enough. In fact, she lived for almost three weeks after her sample was taken. This would have allowed ample time for another sample to be obtained and despatched

.

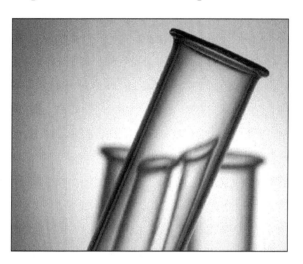

Sample not hypoglycaemic
Mrs. Hall's blood sample was taken at 11.00 am when her blood glucose was normal (i.e. non-hypoglycaemic). The Guildford laboratory's published protocol states the:

crucial, not to say mandatory, requirement is the establishment of hypoglycaemia in the sample submitted for analysis[6]

---

[6] Teale JD, Wark G and Marks V *The biochemical investigation of cases of hypoglycaemia: an assessment of the clinical effectiveness of analytical services.* J Clin Pathol (2002) 55(7): 503–507.

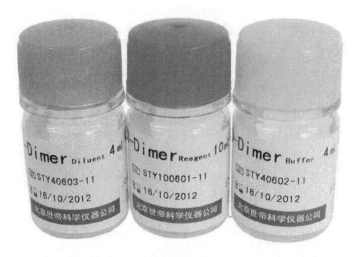

At Colin's trial, the biochemist who conducted the immunoassay on Mrs Hall's blood sample agreed that:

> *to get the best results from the assay the sample should come from a patient who is hypoglycaemic*[7]

He had been willing to conduct the test because the laboratory had been advised that Mrs Hall had received glucose. It remains, however, that the sample sent for analysis was in apparent breach of the laboratory's own procedures.

There are, moreover, factors affecting immunoassays in general which must be taken into account when considering results obtained from such tests:

---

[7] Trial judge's summing up at p193

Interference

The accuracy of immunoassays can be adversely affected by 'interference' caused by the presence of various substances:

The potential for interfering substances to cause inaccurate laboratory results that may cause significant adverse effects on patient care is well known... falsely high or falsely low results may occur[8]

Substances which may cause immunoassay interference are diverse in scope and have been the subject of several large-scale studies[9]. Most interferences originate from components of the sample which interact with assay reagents[10] or the detection system itself. These include *'an interference originating from an additive in a blood collection tube'*.[11] While interference is estimated to occur in less than 2% of immunoassays *'the number of potential errors ... is still high because the number of immunoassays performed is so large'*.

The risk that immunoassays may produce erroneous results can be minimized by conducting more than one test. As noted, this was not done in Mrs Hall's case.

---

[8]Emerson JF and Keane KY *Endogenous Antibody Interferences in Immunoassays* Lab Medicine *(2013) 44:69-73*

[9] see, for example, Marks V *False-positive immunoassay results: a multicenter survey of erroneous immunoassay results from assays of 74 analytes in 10 donors from 66 laboratories in seven countries.* Clin Chem (2002) 48: 2008-2016.

[10] a substance added to a specimen in order to bring about a chemical reaction or to ascertain if a reaction occurs

[11] Kricka LJ and Park JY *Additive-Aggravated Assays: An Authoritative Answer* Clinical Chemistry 51, No. 10, (2005) 1767

No other tests

Immunoassays are almost exclusively carried out for diagnostic – rather than forensic - purposes. More sophisticated and accurate techniques are available.

Methods such as liquid chromatography–mass spectrometry... can be resorted to as comparison methods, especially in forensic and other situations in which absolute identification and accuracy are essential and where erroneous conclusions...may have devastating consequences [12].

Despite the ostensible result on the sample pointing to a possible criminal offence having been committed, it does not appear more sophisticated analytical methods *'available to any well-appointed laboratory'* [13] were ever contemplated.

---

[12] Marks V. op.cit.

[13] ibid

4. Arrest

West Yorkshire Police began interviewing potential witnesses. Their investigation - codenamed Operation Bevel – was headed by **Detective Chief Superintendent Chris Gregg** who 18 months earlier had completed a review of 22 deaths in West Yorkshire associated with serial killer Harold Shipman. Convicted of 15 murders, Shipman is believed to have killed some 250 patients in his care.

West Yorkshire Police found that sixteen LGI staff were working in or near to Ward 36 on the night of 20th November 2002. Among those interviewed were Colin Norris and the other staff nurse who had been on duty with him.

Suspicion

Suspicion fell on Colin when the other staff nurse told police that around midnight he said *'I don't think Ethel looks right'*. He had further allegedly commented *'whenever I do nights someone dies ...it's usually in the mornings... about 5.15 am'*. The staff nurse made little of these remarks having *'heard similar things said before by other colleagues in the past but I didn't think anything unusual about it'*.

The Nurse Practitioner told police Colin Norris said to her *'he had a funny feeling about Ethel'*. Again, she attached no importance to his comment as *'in the nursing profession, people do get feelings about patients and so didn't think it too odd'*.

COLIN NORRIS

Colin Norris was born in Glasgow on 12 February 1976. After leaving school with six GCSEs, he attended a college course in travel and tourism. He worked for several years at travel companies in Glasgow and Stirling before deciding at the age of 22 to switch careers.

In 1998, he applied to study for a Higher Nursing Diploma at Dundee University. He qualified in June 2001 and graduated in October 2001 after which he started work as a staff nurse on Ward 36 at Leeds General Infirmary. In September 2002, he was transferred to another orthopaedic ward at St James's University Hospital in the city as part of a rotation scheme to allow him to gain more experience. He had been unhappy with this move and continued to work individual shifts on Ward 36 at LGI on an agency basis. He was working an agency shift on 20 November 2002.

He had recently purchased a house in Leeds and was generally popular with colleagues. One nurse described him as *'a very good staff nurse'* with a good sense of humour. Another said he was *'a polished member of the team'*. The Health Care Assistant who worked with him on the night Mrs Hall had a hypoglycaemic attack said he was: *'a nice friendly lad. He would do anything for you...had lots of friends outside work and is fun to be with'*.

Prior to his December 2002 arrest, he had never been questioned, charged or convicted in connection with any offence.

Colin Norris

Colin does not recall making the comments to his colleagues but accepts he may have made them in the context of similar conversations often exchanged between hospital nurses.

Arrested
Police arrested Colin at his home on the afternoon of 11th December 2002. He was taken to the Bridewell station in Leeds where he was detained overnight. Police did not begin to interview him until 3.24 pm on the following afternoon.

He was questioned for a total of 4 hours 14 minutes in six separate interviews. The last interview ended at 21.04 following which he was released on police bail. In all, Colin spent 29 hours at the police station.

Det. Ch. Supt. Chris Gregg

Throughout the six interview sessions, he was co-operative and answered all questions put to him. He was accompanied by duty solicitor **Jim Littlehales** who says it *'never came across that he had anything to hide'*. During his first two interviews Colin was asked about his background and work as a nurse. It was only towards the end of third interview (which started at 6.35 pm – more than 24 hours after he was arrested) that police asked him about Ethel Hall. During his final interview, he was asked whether he had injected Mrs. Hall with insulin. He said he had not. The interviewing officer stated:

I'll tell you now the facts...Ethel Hall was administered externally a large, a very large dose of insulin which contributed to her deterioration in health resulting in her death. Fact.

Colin responded:

I just know that, well, I didn't do anything

Colin wanted to know why he had been arrested:

If I hadn't have been working that night or if I hadn't been looking after that team that night then would I be sitting here just now?

The officer replied

If you had not been present in a critical period when we believe drugs were administered, there is a distinct possibility that you would not have been sat there now.

During the 12th December 2002 interviews, the only death about which Colin was questioned was Ethel Hall's. It would be another 16 months before he was quizzed about the deaths of other patients. The reason for his initial arrest appears to have been that Mrs. Hall was in his care when she developed hypoglycaemia and his purported remarks to colleagues earlier that night. Senior officers much later claimed he was arrested because suspicions about other deaths were aired by hospital staff from an early stage. No corroboration for these assertions can be found either in witness statements taken at the time or in trial testimony.

June Morrison

As soon as he was released from custody, Colin telephoned his mother **June Morrison** in Glasgow. She says, he was *'sobbing and couldn't speak...he just could not believe that they had actually arrested him for this'*. A few days later, colleagues arranged a party in a Leeds pub to show their support for him. Immediately after Mrs. Hall died, Colin was suspended from work. He was forced to sell his house in Leeds and moved back to Glasgow as part of his bail conditions.

5. Operation Bevel

Senior officers later expressed the opinion that Colin Norris was *'exceptionally arrogant'* in denying involvement in Ethel Hall's death. The day after he was released on police bail, a meeting was held between the Senior Investigating Officer, Det. Ch. Supt Gregg, his deputy Detective Inspector Martin Hepworth and Leeds Teaching Hospitals Trust staff. It was decided that deaths of patients admitted to wards where Colin had worked (Ward 36 of LGI in 2001/2002 and Ward 23 of St James's University Hospital in 2002) would be examined. The police set the following criteria for deaths which would be treated as *'high priority'* for investigation:

- *All hypoglycaemic incidents resulting in death*

- *Deaths in which the suspect Norris had attended at the time of death or where there was a sudden change in condition*

- *Any other deaths that were suspicious*[14]

From the outset West Yorkshire Police seemingly decided Colin Norris might be a serial killer. At that point, the only concrete evidence against him comprised brief conversations with colleagues (which they regarded as insignificant) and police interviews in which he fully co-operated while denying he murdered Ethel Hall.

---

[14] Hepworth M. *Operation Bevel* op. cit. at p39

DCI Martin Hepworth

A remarkable feature of Operation Bevel was that during almost three years of investigation, police pursued no lines of inquiry into Mrs. Hall's death <u>other</u> than their suspicions against Colin Norris. Investigating officers had accepted at face value the laboratory result which pointed to Mrs. Hall having been injected with insulin. Fifteen other LGI staff also worked in or near Ward 36 on the night in question. It also emerged that hospital security was woeful. Examples included a vagrant found living in a hospital block, drug users' syringes in the grounds and unauthorised intruders regularly being escorted out of the infirmary. At a very early stage, investigating officers seem to have developed 'tunnel vision' as to the expected outcome of their inquiries. Their attention focused exclusively on Colin Norris and their suspicion he was a serial killer.

Investigation

Seventy-two deaths which occurred in the chosen periods were identified for examination. A three page *pro-forma* was completed for each of the deceased with brief information on patient care, whether hypoglycaemia was experienced, whether the patient had diabetes etc. Eighteen cases were classified as 'high priority' for review by a geriatrician, a pharmacologist and a toxicologist. The process by which the cases were selected is unclear but it is reasonable to assume it was based on the criteria set out above which were heavily biased towards cases in which Colin had been involved.

Lucy Rowell

The fundamental flaw in this approach is illustrated by the case of **Lucy Rowell**, an elderly woman with well-controlled diabetes. On 5th February 2002, she was admitted to Ward 36 at LGI with a fractured hip. Some days after her operation, she was moved to another Leeds hospital for physiotherapy. Within hours, she went into a severe hypoglycaemic coma. She was taken back to LGI where she died on 16th March 2002.

Operation Bevel detectives visited Mrs. Rowell's family to advise they were investigating a male nurse on suspicion of causing her death. Eleven months later, police re-visited the family to tell them the investigation into her death had been dropped because the nurse had not been at LGI at the relevant time. Police even produced copies of Colin's work rosters for the date in question. In the words of her granddaughter Miranda Carpenter, Mrs. Rowell's death *'went from suspicious to non-suspicious'*. Having found no connection with Colin, police lost all interest in her death.

Lucy Rowell

Mrs IM

Investigation of another elderly deceased patient IM was also dropped. Mrs. IM was admitted to Ward 23 of St James's Hospital with a fractured femur on 22nd November 2002. Colin was responsible for her overnight care. She was found unresponsive on the morning of 23rd November 2002 and died later that day. Colin was questioned about IM's death in a police interview some 17 months later on 20th April 2004. He denied officers' claims that he was:

> *responsible for the administration of insulin to that lady and responsible for her subsequent death*

At an interview ten months later, Colin was told:

> papers in respect of that case have gone to CPS and they
> advised that at this stage there's insufficient evidence to take
> that any further.

No explanation was ever given for the decision not to charge
Colin in connection with Mrs IM's death.

Other deaths

Hospital records reveal additional instances of hypoglycaemia
in non-diabetic patients on the wards which were not pursued
because they occurred after Colin Norris had been suspended
from work or when he had not been on duty. These included:

Mrs. EW had severe hypoglycaemia in September 2005 and
died after a week. Following *post mortem* examination, a
pathologist stated '*there is no specific pathological evidence to
account for the profound episode of hypoglycaemia*'

Mrs. ML died in 2003 after a severe hypoglycaemic episode
with a reading of 1.1 mmol/L.

Mrs. MH died after Colin Norris was suspended from work.
Nursing notes say MH flopped forward on a commode. Tests
showed her blood glucose level was 0.7 mmol/L She was
given infusions of glucose but did not recover.

Mrs. HO had a blood glucose reading of 0.9 mmol/L[15] on 24th
October 2002 and later died.   Friends of the patient and
hospital staff discussed how sudden and unexpected her
decline was. Colin Norris was not on duty at this time.

---

[15] Prosecution experts discussed prior to Colin's trial, the possibility that the laboratory results on
Mrs HO might be erroneous

Scale

Operation Bevel was one of the largest and longest-running investigations ever mounted by West Yorkshire Police. More than 7200 witness statements were taken during the inquiry. Investigating officers identified over 2300 'nominals' (persons connected with the inquiry) on the HOLMES (Home Office Large Major Enquiry System) computer database. The initial grounds for instituting such a wide-scale investigation focusing on a single individual were apparently tenuous. It would have been a major embarrassment for the force if no-one had been charged after such a costly exercise.

6. Interviews

Colin was questioned (and later charged) in connection with the cases of four patients in addition to Ethel Hall:

Vera Wilby aged 90 was admitted to LGI on 2nd May 2002 with a broken hip. She had high blood pressure and a serious heart condition. On 5th May 2002, surgeons repaired her hip. On 17th May, Mrs. Wilby suffered severe hypoglycaemia with recorded blood glucose levels as low as 1.5 mmol/L. She was given repeated administrations of glucose and survived the episode. She was moved to a nursing home and died in 2003 from unrelated causes. Her remains were cremated.

Bridget Bourke aged 89 was admitted to Ward 36 at LGI on 16th June 2002 after a fall at her home. Her fractured hip was repaired by surgery on 17th June. She suffered a range of conditions having previously had a stroke and treatment for breast cancer. While in Ward 36, she became infected with the bacterium *clostridium difficile*. In the early hours of 21st July 2002, she was found unresponsive by Colin. Her blood sugar was very low. Although glucose was administered, she was found dead on the morning of 22nd July 2002. Mrs Bourke was buried. Her remains were later exhumed but the results of a pathologist's examination were inconclusive.

Doris Ludlam aged 80 was transferred on 12th June 2002 to Ward 36 from another ward at LGI after suffering a fall and breaking her hip. She had various conditions including heart disease and kidney impairment. On 16th June, Mrs. Ludlam was found to have a high blood potassium reading. The usual

top: Bridget Bourke, Ethel Hall, Doris Ludlam
bottom: Vera Wilby, Irene Crooks

treatment for this condition is insulin mixed with glucose. This was administered by Colin Norris on the instructions of a doctor. It was not necessary to give the treatment again. Her hip was repaired by surgery on 21st June 2002. On 25th June, Mrs. Ludlam was found in a hypoglycaemic coma. She died on 27th June 2002. Her remains were cremated.

Irene Crooks aged 78 fractured her hip on 10th October 2002. She was admitted to Ward 23 at St James's Hospital. She had chronic bronchitis and emphysema. Her hip operation took place on 11th October. She was found to be anaemic and received a blood transfusion. In the early hours of 19th

October, Staff Nurse Norris contacted the Nurse Practitioner to say he had just found Mrs. Crooks *'totally unresponsive'*. Blood tests revealed hypoglycaemia. After repeated glucose doses over 12 hours, her blood sugar rose to a high level of 20.4 mmol/L. A doctor instructed she be given insulin. Her blood sugar again fell to a hypoglycaemic level. She died on 20th October 2002. Her remains were cremated.

No blood samples from the women were tested to ascertain what might have caused their hypoglycaemia nor was *post mortem* examination carried out in any of the four cases.

Re-arrested
Following his December 2002 police interviews, Colin was not questioned again until five months later. On 13th May 2003, he was re-arrested and taken to Killingbeck Police Station in Leeds. Colin had been due to attend a police station to answer to bail on 14th May. Despite this, he was arrested at 07.30 am the day before. He was interviewed for a total of 3 hours and 59 minutes in six sessions between 10.50 am and 7.00 pm.

As in his previous interviews, he was only asked about Ethel Hall. Since his arrest, Colin had been suspended from work and lost his home. It was not surprising that he adopted a somewhat more combative attitude during this second series of interviews. At the start of the interview, officers put to him details of the Guildford laboratory test on Mrs. Hall's blood sample for his comments. His solicitor interjected:

> *there's little he can comment on the expert evidence. He's not a medical expert and whilst it can be put to him...my advice to him would be not to answer anything...because clearly he doesn't know and is no expert*

Colin Norris - first police interview

The interviewing officers displayed an incomplete grasp of the scientific evidence as illustrated by the following exchange about the Guildford test:

Officer:	*what he did was dilute that sample by 100 and that would thereby give a more accurate reading*
Colin:	*Dilute it with what?*
Officer:	*He's diluted the sample by 100 and that will give a more accurate reading*
Colin:	*What's he diluted it with?*

| Officer: | *We're just reading out his statement.* |
| | *We're not able to process...* |

| Colin: | *So you don't know.* |

Colin repeatedly asked why he was arrested in December 2002 but the officers failed to answer. He was asked about procedures for handling and administering medication on Ward 36. He answered fully. He was also questioned about lectures he attended at Dundee University on insulin and diabetes. He said he had been at lectures on many topics but hadn't paid much attention. He was asked if he recalled making remarks about Mrs. Hall to colleagues on 20th November 2002. He said he could not remember making the comments but it was possible he had. He pointed out that his colleagues' statements did not – as the officers claimed – suggest he had predicted Mrs. Hall was going to die. He was again released on police bail.

Further interviews
Colin was arrested a further three times over the next ten months. Between December 2002 and October 2005 (when he was charged), he was allowed to retain his passport and travelled abroad – with the full knowledge and permission of police – on several occasions.

On 26th April 2004, he was taken to Killingbeck Police Station for six interview sessions lasting 3 hours and 49 minutes between 10.56 am and 5.05 pm. He was questioned for the first time about the deaths of four patients: Bridget Bourke, Doris Ludlam, Irene Crookes and IM and about Vera Wilby's hypoglycaemia. His solicitor pointed out that the cases dated back two years *'Colin's memory is not going to be that great in relation to what has gone on'.*

The officer conducting the interviews **Det. Sgt. Jane Lemon** later told ITV's *Real Crimes* programme *'what I found very sinister about him was the fact that he couldn't remember these ladies'*. This wasn't correct. Shown a photograph of Vera Wilby, he said he recalled her because of her distinctive hair style. It was put to him that three experts:

> *who have independently examined Mrs. Wilby's notes have said she had a catastrophic hypoglycaemic incident that cannot be explained by normal methods*

He was asked if he injected Mrs. Wilby with insulin which he denied. He again asked for an explanation of his initial arrest:

Colin: *I would just still like some answers as to why I was arrested the first time. Because the first time I got arrested I was told because I was in charge of a team of patients*

Officer: *You're on bail for that and I don't intend to make any comment or answer any questions in relation to a previous arrest.*

Colin: *I've been on bail for about a year and a half and I've still not had an answer. Put yourself in my position that's all I'm saying to you. If you could give me an answer then maybe I could understand a bit better but for the last year and a half, all I keep getting told is because I was in charge of a team of patients. None of all this stuff had come to light at that point. As far as you was concerned, I was in charge of a team of patients, a patient died, it was a murder investigation. All this time on suspicion of murder – eighteenmonths down the line I'm still in the same position.*

The officers refused to answer. He was then asked about Doris Ludlam who had been admitted to LGI almost two years previously. Colin did not recognise her from her photograph and could not recall her case. Despite this, officers questioned him about her care and administration of pain relief over several hours culminating in asking him

Officer: *Did you murder Doris Ludlam?*

Colin: *No*

Officer: *Try to kill Doris Ludlam?*

Colin: *No. Where's the stuff about how long it takes for the blood sugar?*

Earlier in the interview, Colin asked if the officers knew how long after an insulin injection it would take for blood sugar *'to get so low that it doesn't register a reading'*. In Mrs. Ludlam's case, his work rosters showed he was not on duty when her hypoglycaemia was detected. The officers confirmed they had such information and suspended the interview so they could *'have a look now'* at the experts' advice. On resumption of the interview, the officers made no further mention of this evidence and proceeded to question him about Bridget Bourke, Irene Crookes and IM. He did not recognise them from photographs shown to him. He pointed out *'they're in hospital...it's hard to imagine them when they're not sedated'*. He did, however, recall a female patient who died at St James's Hospital who was probably Mrs. IM. He said he might be able to remember more if officers could supply further details about her. He could also recall a patient in *'Bed 16'* who was probably Mrs. Crookes albeit that *'I don't remember much about her'*. The officers gave hardly any information about the patients to assist Colin's memory but then asked in respect of each woman whether he injected them with insulin. He replied in the negative. He was again released on police bail.

Jim Littlehales

Fourth arrest

On 15th September 2004, Colin was questioned for a fourth time. He was interviewed in four sessions lasting 2 hours and 44 minutes between 10.15 am and 1.20 pm. He was only questioned about Mrs. Bourke's death and quizzed in detail about procedures and security in Ward 36.

He was again shown a photograph of Mrs. Bourke. He acknowledged he had written various notes about her in hospital records but repeated that he could not recall her specifically. It was put to him that experts believed Mrs. Bourke had received insulin by external injection which caused her hypoglycaemia.

Detectives queried his inability to recall Mrs. Bourke. Colin attempted to explain that deaths of elderly patients on the

ward were not uncommon and considerable time had
passed since Mrs. Bourke's demise:

Colin: *You see if I'd been asked about it at the time, I
would have been able to answer your questions
just like that but I mean you're asking me stuff
two years ago, what I thought two years ago.
That's like saying to you, do you remember that
guy you interviewed two years ago for burgling
a house?*

DS Lemon: *We don't want to get into an argument about
what we might do or he might do. If somebody
said to me, do you remember interviewing that
man about a murder three years ago, I think I'd
be able to remember quite a bit.*

Colin: *Murder's slightly different from burgling a
house. That's why I used that as an example. It's
just like something every day. You probably deal
with burglary every day.*

DS Lemon's interview with ITV's *Real Crimes* took place
shortly after Colin's conviction. In light of the above
exchange, her inability to recall that Colin had remembered
- even after two years - details of some of the women was
perhaps ironic. He was yet again released on police bail.

Final interviews
Colin's final police interviews took place on 23rd February
2005. Three interview sessions lasted 2 hours and 2 minutes
between 11.08 am and 1.22 pm.

Det. Sgt. Jane Lemon

At the commencement of the interviews, he was informed he would be asked no more questions about Mrs. IM's death. The Crown Prosecution Service had advised there *'was insufficient evidence to take that any further'*. He was not told why the investigation into her death had been halted or how her case differed from the other five.

His solicitor reiterated that Colin was unable to comment on expert evidence. The officers outlined experts' views that the women had suffered hypoglycaemia as a result of insulin injection. He was asked again about procedures on the ward for handling insulin. Officers continued to challenge - at considerable length - Colin's inability to recall some of the patients about whom he was being questioned:

DS Lemon: *I'm not going to read out all the statements because it, it'd just take forever but it's fair to say that your colleagues in the hospital whether they are consultants or doctors or nursing staff, even students, seem to have a better recollection of these ladies than you do. Can you offer any explanation for that?*

The officer's assertion that other staff remembered more than Colin was not *'fair to say'*. Examination of statements made by medical and nursing staff who cared for the women confirms the substantial majority could not recall them and had to consult records completed at the time in order to make their statements.

In his final interview, Colin repeated *'I never killed anyone'*.

On 12th October 2005, he was charged with murdering Ethel Hall, Bridget Bourke, Doris Ludlam and Irene Crookes and the attempted murder of Vera Wilby. He was remanded in custody. In March 2006, he was released on conditional bail. It took more than two years from the time Colin was charged for the Crown to bring its case to trial.

7. Trial

Colin's trial opened at Newcastle Crown Court on 16th October 2007 before Mr. Justice Griffiths-Williams. Colin was represented by William Harbage QC while Robert Smith QC appeared for the Crown. The trial was long and complex lasting 19 weeks. The trial judge's summing-up of the evidence runs to 524 pages and took a week to deliver.

Over 80 witnesses gave evidence for the prosecution. They largely comprised medical and scientific experts, doctors and nursing staff. Written statements from a further 38 prosecution witnesses were entered in evidence by agreement with the defence. Twelve witnesses including Colin were called for the defence and two written statements entered.

Apart from the brief testimony of Det. Sgt. Lemon, no senior police officers gave evidence. The jury consequently received next to no information about the process by which deaths in the hospitals were selected for investigation, why certain cases were not included, the methodology adopted during the lengthy police inquiry and the reasons for Colin's initial arrest.

The prosecution case rested on two main propositions that:

- the result on Ethel Hall's blood sample showed she was injected with a large external dose of insulin causing fatal hypoglycaemia

- the other women's hypoglycaemia was very rare and only explicable by the administration of insulin or other diabetes medication.

The *'common denominator'*, argued the Crown, was Colin who was on duty at or around the time the women developed hypoglycaemia.

In support of their case, the Crown claimed Colin told *'clear lies'* in his first interview. It was alleged he had predicted the time of Mrs. Hall's death. The prosecution purported to show that Colin disliked elderly people. It was further claimed that insulin kept on Ward 36 had gone missing around the time of Mrs. Hall's hypoglycaemic attack (albeit that hospital staff could not recall how much insulin was in the ward refrigerator over the preceding three nights).

The defence submitted there was no evidence of unlawful insulin injections to four of the women and that Crown experts lacked direct experience of the patients. Concerning Mrs. Hall, the defence challenged the laboratory result and also postulated the possibility that an unauthorised person may have entered the ward on the night in question[16].

The Experts
Much of the trial was devoted to testimony from medical and scientific experts. The normal rule in criminal trials is that witnesses may only testify about facts within their direct experience. Their opinions about those facts may not be admitted in evidence. The exception to this rule is evidence from experts who possess special knowledge or skill beyond that of the average person. Expert witnesses may offer opinions within their field of expertise.

---

[16] Colin himself has never believed that any such person was in the ward.

Sixteen expert witnesses were called by the Crown. The prosecution experts included a consultant geriatrician, a pharmacologist and those with expertise in chemistry, diabetes, cardiology, neuropathology, stroke, forensic pathology, biochemistry, tumours and radiology.

The defence called five expert witnesses: a consultant biochemist, forensic pathologist, cancer specialist, geriatrician and diabetes specialist

The Guildford result

Various possible causes of Ethel Hall's hypoglycaemia were ruled out including insulinoma – a rare tumour of the pancreas. The expert evidence about her death largely depended on the validity of tests on the blood sample taken on 20th November 2002. The head of the Guildford laboratory said he was *'absolutely convinced of the veracity of the results'*.

Guildford laboratory result
• C-peptide test not carried out for five days.
• No second assay after highly unusual initial result.
• No antibody test to exclude/confirm Insulin Autoimmune Syndrome.
• Second sample not requested despite ample time.
• Level below which c-peptide deemed non-measurable not accepted by other laboratories.
• No analytical method other than immunoassay used.
• Possibility of 'interference' from additive in blood collection tube or other source.

Insulin Autoimmune Syndrome

Assisting biochemist Dr Gwen Wark accepted that antibody tests to exclude Insulin Autoimmune Syndrome had not been run. She said there was no IAS because there was a high level of insulin and an absence of C-peptide. This was a dubious conclusion. A study of a rare IAS case found *'C-peptide was disproportionately low in comparison to insulin levels'*[17].

Despite confirming that the apparent amount of insulin in Mrs. Hall's sample was one of the highest the laboratory had ever recorded, Dr Wark claimed *'there was no need to repeat as the result was consistent with the administration of insulin'*.[18]

---

[17] Kasznicki et al *A case of recurrent, spontaneous postprandial and fasting hypoglycemia and insulin autoantibodies in a patient with coexisting Graves' disease, megaloblastic anemia, and multiple myeloma.* 2011. Dlevliabet Dośw Klin 11, 2: 103–105 at p105

[18] Trial judge' summing up at p194

For the defence, consultant biochemist **Dr Adel Ismail** said the way to distinguish between hypoglycaemia due to insulin injection and IAS is to run a 'polyethylene glycol test'. This was not done.

He further said the tests carried out by the Guildford laboratory were misleading as the level below which the laboratory claimed c-peptide could not be detected was not generally accepted. Other laboratories adopt a lower measure.

Dr Adel Ismail

He said results from assay tests can be falsely high or low and are therefore unpredictable and prone to interference. In his view, the result on Mrs. Hall's sample fitted more closely with IAS. Studies had concluded that pernicious anaemia - an autoimmune disease from which Mrs. Hall suffered for many years – is a strong predisposing factor in IAS.

The experts were invited to consider a reported instance of IAS known as the 'Cambridge case'[19] which had also featured a high insulin level with low c-peptide. The Guildford biochemist said the Cambridge case was not relevant because low(rather than no) c-peptide had been found in that case (albeit that the level at which c-peptide was considered by the Guildford laboratory not to be measurable was challenged).

A prosecution endocrinologist claimed IAS only causes mild hypoglycaemia easily controlled by eating something sweet. This latter statement was incorrect as confirmed by – among others - the Cambridge case in which the patient's profound *'hypoglycemia could only be reversed by iv[20] 50% dextrose infusion'[21].*

No doubts
Consultant geriatrician, **Dr Peter Kroker** said the prospect of a patient contracting IAS is *'probably less than winning the lottery'.* He gave no estimate of the odds against a patient being murdered by insulin injection.

Consultant pharmacologist **Professor Robin Ferner** testified he had *'absolutely no doubt'* Mrs. Hall's low blood glucose level when she was found unresponsive was caused by massive insulin injection.

---

[19] Halsall et al *Hypoglycemia due to an insulin binding antibody in a patient with an IgA-kappa myeloma* J.Clin.Endocrinol Metab 2007 Jun;92(6):2013-6

[20] intravenous

[21] Halsall et al *op. cit*

Professor Robin Ferner

Non-diabetic hypoglycaemia

A blood plasma test and immediate *post mortem* examination had only been carried out in Mrs. Hall's case. The Crown's claim that Vera Wilby, Bridget Bourke, Doris Ludlam and Irene Crookes were injected with insulin was based on inferences drawn from blood sugar charts and other clinical information. The contention that '*severe hypoglycaemia in non-diabetics is very rare*'[22] was crucial to the prosecution case. Professor Ferner said it would be '*very extraordinary*' to find five such cases in such a time span. There was no clinically explicable cause for the patients' hypoglycaemia, he stated, other than the administration of large doses of insulin or other diabetes medication.

---

[22] Trial judge's summing up at p1

Exhumation

Mrs. Bourke's body was exhumed on 30th September 2003 some 14 months after her burial. Decomposition had taken place and her body was in a poor condition. No evidence of a pancreatic tumour was found. A prosecution pathologist gave his opinion that her death was caused by hypoglycaemic coma due to insulin injection. Challenged by the defence why he believed her low blood sugar was the result of insulin injection, he said this was the most plausible explanation.

Mrs. BD

The defence submitted the case of an LGI patient, **Mrs. BD**, a 73 year old woman found with severe hypoglycaemia before Colin started work at the hospital and while he was still a student at Dundee University almost 300 miles away. Mrs. BD had diabetes which was controlled by diet alone. She did not take any diabetes medication. When her blood sugar level rose, she was given a very small amount of insulin in five separate doses. Her blood chart showed she became severely hypoglycaemic over a twelve hour period (falling as low as 1.1 mmol/L) for which glucose was administered.

The defence argued that Mrs. BD's severe hypoglycaemia could not be explained by the small documented amount of insulin she had received. Experts differed in their interpretation of her clinical records. A prosecution endocrinologist accepted she may have been given more insulin than had been recorded which would, he agreed, have amounted to a *malicious act*.

Despite Mrs BD having similar symptoms to the women who Colin was accused of having murdered, the prosecution claimed that Mrs BD died of natural causes.

Prediction of death

The Crown placed great emphasis on the statement of the staff nurse on duty with Colin when Mrs. Hall was found hypoglycaemic. The prosecution alleged he had predicted the time of Mrs. Hall's death. According to the staff nurse, Colin allegedly said:

Whenever I do nights, someone always dies

and slightly later

It's usually in the morning when things go wrong, about 5.15 am'.

The staff nurse had

heard similar things said before by other colleagues in the past, but I didn't think anything unusual about it'.

Mrs. Hall did not die at 5.15 am on 20th December 2002 but some three weeks later. The misconception underlying the Crown's assertion was the notion that it is possible to gauge accurately the timing and effect of insulin injection. Several experts testified that insulin acts differently between persons and even within the same individual at different times. It would be impossible for anyone to predict the time of death in the manner described.

Clear Lies?

The prosecution claimed Colin told *'clear lies'* in his first police interviews when asked about his knowledge of hypoglycaemia. He had said all he had done was to give patients sugary food and drink. In the cases of Mrs. Wilby, Mrs. Bourke and Mrs. Crookes he had taken blood sugar tests and administered glucose. This showed, the Crown alleged, that he lied to deflect attention from cases other than Mrs. Hall. The interview transcript confirms he merely commented he had not conducted a particular procedure which involves rubbing dextrose gel on the inside of patients' cheeks (the five women were given glucose intravenously). His reference to sugary food/drink related to mild hypoglycaemia where patients were conscious.

Insulin stocks

The Crown claimed vials of insulin amounting to 1000 units went missing from Ward 36 around the time Mrs. Hall developed hypoglycaemia. The defence pointed to major deficiencies in stocktaking of non-controlled medications (which include insulin) and record keeping at the hospital rendering such a claim highly uncertain. Moreover, no staff members on duty between 4.40 pm on 18th November and 6.00 am on 20th November 2002 had actually observed how much (or how little) insulin was in the ward refrigerator.

Painkillers

The use of analgesic medication is commonplace on orthopaedic wards before and after surgery. Patients receive painkillers according to prescriptions and a 'pain ladder' authorised by a doctor. The Crown claimed that Colin injected Vera Wilby and Doris Ludlam with morphine or diamorphine which they did not need. His intention, the Crown claimed, was to make the women drowsy so they would raise no objection to subsequent unlawful insulin injection.

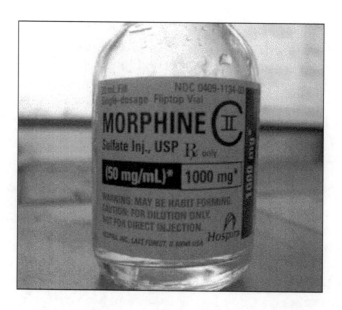

There were contradictions in the prosecution's argument. In both instances, the analgesic was administered in conjunction with a female staff nurse (who would effectively have acted as an accomplice if the injection was unnecessary). While the records were unclear, it was possible the drug was injected by the other nurse. Morphine and diamorphine are controlled drugs subject to much tighter stock-keeping than insulin. None had gone missing during the periods in question. The prosecution speculated that Colin might have prised open the hospital 'sharps bin' in which used syringes were deposited and extracted any remaining morphine from them.

The Crown neglected to explain why a patient might resist an unlawful insulin injection but would not object to an injection of an analgesic which they had not requested.

Nursing elderly patients
The prosecution claimed Colin was motivated by dislike of elderly patients. The Crown pointed to his 12th December 2002

police interview in which he said he found bathing and tending to older female patients difficult while on student placement. He had, however, made clear he only had such problems *'at first'* and *'soon got over it'*. At his trial, he denied any dislike of older patients commenting *'if you do not like elderly patients you should not be in nursing'*.

Colin's testimony

Colin gave evidence over several days answering questions on the many issues which arose during the trial. During cross-examination, Robert Smith QC put to him :

you were going to carry on killing elderly patients in your care by a technique you were still perfecting

Colin replied:

I can't really carry on killing when I haven't killed in the first place

Mr Smith asked if Colin felt surprise when Mrs. Crookes was found in a coma. He replied:

No I didn't...patients in hospital wards deteriorate in health on a regular basis, it is not something that stands out

It was asserted:
you were becoming increasingly confident in your ability to kill patients and not be detected

Colin answered

No sir, I have never killed anyone so how could I become more confident?

Guilty

Such was the trial's length and complexity that Griffiths-Williams J. took five days to read out his summing-up to the jury . Much of it was devoted to the scientific and medical evidence from 21 expert witnesses. The jurors retired to consider their verdict on 27th February 2008. Their deliberations lasted five days culminating in the trial judge advising them that they could deliver a majority verdict.

On 3rd March 2008 – by an 11 to 1 majority – the jury returned a guilty verdict.

On 4th March 2004, he received a life sentence with a recommendation that he serve a minimum 30 years in prison. Sentencing Colin, Mr Justice Griffiths-Williams described him as:

an arrogant and manipulative man with a real dislike of elderly patients… Despite months of evidence, I am no wiser as to your motive… You are, I have absolutely no doubt, a thoroughly evil and dangerous man.

Immediately after the jury's verdict, DCS Chris Gregg who led Operation Bevel claimed that for Colin:

even throwing blankets off the bed would be sufficient for him to kill …it was the level of difficulty they were presenting to him which frustrated him - which is similar to Harold Shipman…Norris took the opportunity to murder people just to satisfy his own frustrations and limitations. He is on a short fuse and anything that slightly agitated him, he responded by killing people with lethal doses.

Mr Justice Griffiths-Williams

DCS Gregg had never met let alone interviewed Colin. There is nothing in the transcripts of Colin's police interviews or statements made about him by others which provides any factual basis for DCS Gregg's speculations.

8. Appeal

Colin's appeal against conviction took place at the Royal Courts of Justice on 9th December 2009. He was represented by **William Clegg QC** and **Jeffrey Samuels QC** while the Crown was represented by the original trial counsel.

Colin's grounds of appeal were that the trial judge failed to direct the jury adequately on 'cross admissibility' of evidence concerning the cause of hypoglycaemia suffered by the five women and the identity of the alleged perpetrator i.e. the extent to which the jury could take account of evidence concerning one or more of the five women in determining the facts in the other cases.

After reviewing the trial evidence and the summing-up, the Court of Appeal ruled there had been no misdirection to the jury. Colin's conviction was upheld.

9. New Evidence

The key evidence repeated frequently at trial (and accepted by both prosecution and defence) was the contention that *'severe hypoglycaemia in non-diabetics is very rare*[23]*'*.

Defence expert **Dr David Cohen** agreed *'it is extraordinary to find five cases'*. While the jury clearly took great care over its deliberations, the experts' unanimity on this question must have featured prominently in the decision of the majority to find Colin Norris guilty.

In 2011, **Professor Vincent Marks**, widely acknowledged as the world's leading expert on insulin poisoning, prepared a report for Colin's new solicitor, **Jeremy Moore**. His findings were remarkable based on his own extensive knowledge and expertise coupled with a review of new medical research studies conducted world-wide since 2008 into the hitherto under-researched incidence of spontaneous hypoglycaemia among non-diabetic hospital patients. Professor Marks concluded that the phenomenon is relatively common. Far from being extremely rare, spontaneous hypoglycaemia affects 5% to 10% of non-diabetic elderly patients with risk factors including other serious conditions (as was the case with all of the women).

It was, therefore, unsurprising that investigation of patients on the two orthopaedic wards found four such cases. In

---

[23] Trial judge's summing up at p1

this context, there exists no evidence that any of the four women were injected with insulin.

Professor Vincent Marks

In Mrs Hall's case, Professor Marks said he believes someone had given her insulin at some time which would explain the clinical picture and the laboratory results.

However, in an October 2011 film *A Jury in the Dark* made for BBC Scotland by former BBC *Rough Justice* producer **Louise Shorter** (now of Inside Justice) and journalist **Mark Daly**, Dr Adel Ismail (who gave evidence for the defence at Colin's trial) pointed to a further problem with assays such as that carried out on Mrs. Hall's blood sample. In the United Kingdom, he said, *'one in every 250 results can be erroneous'*. He criticised the fact that only one blood sample was taken from Mrs. Hall. Professor Marks agreed it was *'a great shame she was not investigated more thoroughly'.*

Mark Daly in *A Jury in the Dark*

Other recent studies unconnected with Colin's case have repeated Professor Marks' findings. In April 2012, a team from the Department of Elderly Medicine at Rotherham General Hospital and Beds & Herts Postgraduate Medical School published *Hypoglycaemia in hospitalized non-diabetic older people*[24]. The paper reviewed recent studies while noting a previous *'paucity of literature regarding the incidence of hypoglycaemia in non-diabetic patients'*[25]. The review found that *'hypoglycaemia is not uncommon in hospitalized non-diabetic older people'* with other serious conditions.

---

[24] Abdelhafiz et al *Hypoglycaemia in hospitalized non-diabetic older people* European Geriatric Medicine 3 (2012) 174-178

[25] Ibid at p174

Likewise an Italian research study in 2006[26] found that 8.6% of older non-diabetic patients admitted to hospital during the study period developed hypoglycaemia[27] on one or more occasions during their hospital stay.

When an appeal against conviction has been dismissed, a further appeal hearing can usually only be secured by referral from the Criminal Cases Review Commission (CCRC), the body empowered to investigate alleged miscarriages of justice. In most cases, the CCRC will only refer cases if fresh evidence casting doubt on the safety of the conviction emerges which was not capable of being raised at the trial or previous appeals.

Jeremy Moore

[26] Mannucci et al *Incidence and prognostic significance of hypoglycaemia in hospitalized non-diabetic patients* Ageing Clin. Exp. Res. 18: 446-451 2006

[27] Ibid at p448

Representations detailing the new evidence in Colin's case were submitted to the Commission in late 2011 by his solicitor Jeremy Moore. In 2012, the Commission advised it would conduct a full investigation into Colin's case. Given the complexity of the case and the massive amount of evidential material which must be examined, it is likely the CCRC's inquiry will take some considerable time before it decides whether or not Colin's conviction will be referred to the Court of Appeal.

10. Conclusion

At Colin's trial, prosecution biochemist **Professor Alexander Forrest** correctly observed that a scientific hypothesis can never be proved conclusively. Scientists can only find data which may or may not be consistent with the hypothesis. Despite popular belief in the notion of 'exact' science, no such certainty can exist. Even as recently as 2008, conventional medical and scientific opinion – as expressed by the experts at Colin's trial - was that severe hypoglycaemia among non-diabetic patients is very rare. Current research casts serious doubt on that hypothesis. Had jurors been aware that the phenomenon is relatively common, it is hard to envisage how they could have returned a guilty verdict. Even if issues surrounding the laboratory result on Ethel Hall's blood sample are ignored or set aside, there was no evidence on which Colin could have plausibly been charged with her murder without the cases of the other four women.

The adversarial nature of the English trial system encourages some expert witnesses to adopt a 'clear cut' dogmatic stance rather than offering more qualified, tentative opinions which may leave jurors confused and/or unimpressed. The trial judge in Colin's case correctly warned jurors that the expert witnesses had put forward opinions but it is nevertheless possible the persistent false belief in scientific certainty prevailed. After five months of complex expert evidence, jurors may well have been 'blinded by science'.

The extensive police inquiry was flawed from the outset. Based on little more than guesswork, a large, costly inquiry was instituted. The apparent manner in which the deaths of patients in Wards 36 and 23 were selected for investigation lends support to the notion that police (in the words of Colin's solicitor) *cherry-picked those cases when Colin Norris was on duty*. At least one investigation into a supposedly suspicious death in which Colin could not have been involved was dropped. No other lines of inquiry were pursued.

Following Colin's conviction, repeated comparisons were made by senior officers with the case of Harold Shipman. This extended to portraying Colin as a 'loner'. In reality, he was gregarious and popular with patients and colleagues. Police also implied his co-operation during interviews was probative of an arrogant and manipulative personality.

Stepping Hill
A parallel with Colin's case arose in 2011 in the investigation into alleged insulin poisoning at Stepping Hill Hospital, Stockport. Greater Manchester Police (who were strongly criticised for their failures in the Shipman case) arrested staff nurse **Rebecca Leighton**. She was charged with criminal damage with intent to endanger life and recklessness as to whether life would be endangered. Displaying a distinct poverty of imagination, tabloid journalists also dubbed her the *'Angel of Death'*[28]. Ms. Leighton's Facebook page in which – like millions of others – she sometimes complained about her work was used to portray her as a 'party girl' who disliked patients. Just six weeks after her arrest, all charges against her were dropped. Greater Manchester Police then began investigating another male nurse who has been

---

[28] *Stepping Hill nurse blames media for 'angel of death' ordeal* The Times 20 September 2011

interviewed and released on police bail several times. In January 2013, the *Daily Star* newspaper reported that despite 65 officers working full time on the inquiry for (by then) 18 months, an anonymous police source said the case

> *just isn't ready for charges to happen. The longer the process goes on, you wonder if it's a matter of going back to the drawing board*[29]

Colin with his grandmother Elizabeth Ogilvie

Colin's case gives rise to serious concern about the manner in which such inquiries are approached both by police and health authorities in the post-Shipman era. Many agencies were responsible for serious failures to stop Harold Shipman before he had killed at least 250 patients. The grave errors of the past, however, will not be corrected by the conviction of innocent people for 'murders' which never happened.

---

[29] *Hospital murders suspect won't be charged* Daily Star 6 January 2013

11. What you can do

- Join the support group for Colin by emailing: freecolinnorris@aol.com

- Ask your trade/student union, community group, church, political party or other body to adopt Colin's case and to invite speakers from the support group.

- Write to Colin letting him know you support his campaign for justice:

Colin Campbell[30]
A4241AE
A Wing
H M Prison Frankland
Brasside
Durham
DH1 5YD

- Make a donation to the support group (cheques payable to Colin Norris Support Group c/o Inside Justice, Botley Mills,Botley, Southampton, Hampshire SO30 2GB). All funds are used to publicise Colin's case and for no other purpose

---

[30] Colin changed his surname by deed poll some years ago. He prefers to be called Colin Campbell. He was charged and convicted under his birth name and has been referred under this name in this booklet.

12. Inside Justice

Inside Justice was launched in July 2010 to investigate alleged miscarriages of justice. We work with solicitors and other legal representatives and encourage collaboration with external organisations.

Inside Justice is led by Louise Shorter who for 10 years was a producer/director of the BBC's miscarriage of justice series *Rough Justice.* Our core strength comes from our Advisory Panel of experts from a rich range of disciplines. The panel considers cases put before them with a view to identifying new work and investigative strands. We have a budget to commission new forensic work on individual cases and strive to support and facilitate academic research on key issues affecting the criminal justice system.

The unit is a division of *Inside Time* and was established with charitable funding from the Esmée Fairbairn Foundation, the Michael Newsum Charitable Trust, the Roddick Foundation and *Inside Time.*

website: www.insidetime.org/justice-home.asp

email: ls@insidetime.org

Printed in Great Britain
by Amazon.co.uk, Ltd.,
Marston Gate.